BEARPORT BIOG

QUEEN ELIZABETH II

RECORD-BREAKING ROYAL

by Rachel Rose

BEARPORT
PUBLISHING

Minneapolis, Minnesota

Credits

Cover and title page, © Max Mumby/Indigo/Getty Images; 4, © ZGPhotography/Shutterstock; 5, © WPA Pool/Pool/Getty Images; 6, © Lisa Sheridan/Stringer/Getty Images; 7, © Hulton Deutsch/Contributor/Getty Images; 8, © Dave Porter/Shutterstock; 9, © Begoon/Wikimedia; 10, © Cecil Beaton/Wikimedia; 11, © Popperfoto/Contributor/Getty Images; 12, © Keystone/Stringer/Getty Images; 13, © Hulton Deutsch/Contributor/Getty Images; 14, © JANE BARLOW/Contributor/Getty Images; 15, © PA Images/Contributor/Getty Images; 17, © Tim Graham/Contributor/Getty Images; 18, © Tim Graham/Contributor/Getty Images; 19, © Pool/Tim Graham Picture LIbrary/Getty Images; 20, © Featureflash Photo Agency/Shutterstock; 21, © Nagualdesign/Wikimedia

Bearport Publishing Company Product Development Team

President: Jen Jenson; Director of Product Development: Spencer Brinker; Senior Editor: Allison Juda; Editor: Charly Haley; Associate Editor: Naomi Reich; Senior Designer: Colin O'Dea; Associate Designer: Elena Klinkner; Associate Designer: Kayla Eggert; Product Development Assistant: Anita Stasson

Library of Congress Cataloging-in-Publication Data

Names: Rose, Rachel, 1968- author.
Title: Queen Elizabeth II : record-breaking royal / by Rachel Rose.
Other titles: Queen Elizabeth the Second
Description: Minneapolis, Minnesota : Bearport Publishing Company, [2023] | Series: Bearport biographies | Includes bibliographical references and index.
Identifiers: LCCN 2022043634 (print) | LCCN 2022043635 (ebook) | ISBN 9798885094061 (library binding) | ISBN 9798885095280 (paperback) | ISBN 9798885096430 (ebook)
Subjects: LCSH: Elizabeth II, Queen of Great Britain, 1926-2022--Juvenile literature. | Queens--Great Britain--Biography--Juvenile literature.
Classification: LCC DA590 .R67 2023 (print) | LCC DA590 (ebook) | DDC 941.085092 [B]--dc23/eng/20220909
LC record available at https://lccn.loc.gov/2022043634
LC ebook record available at https://lccn.loc.gov/2022043635

For more information, write to Bearport Publishing, 5357 Penn Avenue South, Minneapolis, MN 55419.

Contents

A Royal Celebration

Queen Elizabeth II stood on the **balcony** of Buckingham Palace surrounded by her family. Airplanes zoomed overhead and the roar of their engines was met with cheers from the crowds below. It was all part of a big **celebration**. Elizabeth had been queen for 70 years!

As queen, Elizabeth was a **symbol** of the United Kingdom. She didn't make laws. Her **parliament** did.

The Palace of Westminster is where the British Parliament meets.

The big 70-year celebration kicked off on June 2, 2022.

The Princess Years

Elizabeth Alexandra Mary Windsor was born on April 21, 1926, in London, England. Her mother and father were a **duchess** and **duke**. Elizabeth and her younger sister, Margaret, were princesses. They grew up in a 25-bedroom home, where the sisters would play and have their school lessons.

As a child, Elizabeth's nickname was Lilibet because she wasn't able to say her full name.

Growing up, Elizabeth loved playing with the family dogs.

Elizabeth *(right)* with her sister *(middle)* and her grandmother, Queen Mary *(left)*

When Elizabeth was 10, her whole life changed. Her father became the king of the United Kingdom. That meant Elizabeth would one day become the queen. Right away, she began working hard to learn all the things a **future** queen should know. The history of her country became one of her favorite subjects. Elizabeth was excited to serve her people one day.

Elizabeth and her family moved to Buckingham Palace when her father became king.

Elizabeth's father wasn't supposed to be king. He got the job after his brother decided not to take the throne.

Elizabeth's childhood changed again in 1939 when World War II began. Along with many other children, the princess was sent to live safely outside London. Still, she knew of the war that raged all over Europe. When she turned 19, Elizabeth wanted to do her part. She joined the British army and trained to be a **mechanic**.

During WWII, Elizabeth wrote letters to her old friend, Philip Mountbatten. After the war ended, the two got married.

Princess Elizabeth learned to fix and drive trucks in the army.

The Queen's Job

A few years after leaving the army, Elizabeth's father died. It was her time to become queen. On June 2, 1953, the 27-year-old was crowned Queen Elizabeth II. She was now the head of the United Kingdom and six **Commonwealth** nations.

Over time, the Commonwealth grew. Elizabeth eventually became queen of 15 nations, including the United Kingdom.

As queen, a large part of Elizabeth's job was traveling to other countries. She took her first Commonwealth tour in 1953. For six months, she traveled to different places in the countries she ruled. Then, four years later, Elizabeth made her first official visit to the United States. Throughout her time as queen, Elizabeth visited more than 110 countries!

Queen Elizabeth kept track of what was going on at home, too. She got reports from the British Parliament every day.

Elizabeth with Liz Truss, the leader of Parliament

Elizabeth and Philip traveled by ship
during her first Commonwealth tour.

Supporting **charities** was another important part of Elizabeth's role as queen. She gave time and money to more than 600 groups. Some of her favorite charities helped young children get a good education. The Queen's support meant a lot. The causes she championed raised about 1.4 billion pounds every year. That's about $2 billion.

Elizabeth gave a lot of money to help people during natural disasters all around the world.

Sometimes, Queen Elizabeth met with students through her charity work.

17

Queen of Firsts

Throughout her rule, Elizabeth **challenged** the way the royal family did things. When she was crowned, she asked for the event to be shown on television so everyone could watch. In 1970, she was the first British queen or king to walk in crowds and shake hands with her people. Elizabeth wanted to be more approachable to those she served.

Elizabeth loved to spend her spare time with her corgis and horses.

Elizabeth had more than 30 corgis throughout her life.

Queen Elizabeth wanted to know her people, and she wanted her people to know her.

Leaving a Legacy

Queen Elizabeth II led her people with a strong sense of duty until her death on September 8, 2022. She traveled far and wide, representing Britain all over the world. From her first day as queen to the end of her life, Elizabeth worked hard to bring the royal family closer to the people they serve. Elizabeth leaves the **legacy** of a queen who cared deeply for her people.

Elizabeth was a queen longer than any other king or queen in the history of the United Kingdom.

Queen Elizabeth II · 1926–2022

Timeline

Here are some key dates in Queen Elizabeth II's life.

1926

Born on
April 21

1936

Her father
becomes king

1945

Joins the
British army

1947

Marries
Prince Philip

1953

Crowned
queen

1970

First walk among
her people

2022

Celebrates 70 years
as queen

2022

Dies on
September 8

Glossary

balcony a platform surrounded by railings on the outside of a building

celebration a gathering for a special event

challenged questioned if something was right or not

charities groups that try to help people in need

Commonwealth a group of states or nations that are led by the same ruler

duchess a woman who holds the rank below a princess in the United Kingdom

duke a man who holds the rank below a prince in the United Kingdom

future a time that has not happened yet

legacy something left by a person in the past

mechanic a person who works to fix machines, such as cars and trucks

parliament a group of people who have been elected to make laws in the United Kingdom

symbol someone or something that represents something larger

Index

Read More

Stine, Megan. *Who Is Queen Elizabeth II? (Who Was?)*. New York: Penguin Workshop, 2021.

Williams, Brenda and Brian. *Queen Elizabeth II (DK Life Stories)*. New York: DK Publishing, 2020.

Learn More Online

1. Go to **www.factsurfer.com** or scan the QR code below.

2. Enter "**Queen Elizabeth II**" into the search box.

3. Click on the cover of this book to see a list of websites.

About the Author

Rachel Rose is a writer who lives in San Francisco. Her favorite books to write are about people who lead inspiring lives.